The Underwater
Alphabet Book

by Jerry Pallotta

Illustrated by Edgar Stewart

Jerry says thank you to Paul and Marie Harrigan.
To Annie Stewart, for her love and her help with all the fish.
Also, thank you to H. J. Walker, Jr. of Scripps Institution of Oceanography.

Books by Jerry Pallotta:
The Icky Bug Alphabet Book, The Bird Alphabet Book,
The Ocean Alphabet Book, The Flower Alphabet Book,
The Yucky Reptile Alphabet Book, The Frog Alphabet Book,
The Furry Alphabet Book, The Dinosaur Alphabet Book,
The Underwater Alphabet Book, Going Lobstering

Copyright © 1991 by Jerry Pallotta
Illustrations Copyright © 1991 by Edgar Stewart
Library of Congress Catalog Card Number 91-070015
ISBN 0-88106-455-6 (softcover)   ISBN 0-88106-461-0 (hardcover)
Published by Charlesbridge Publishing, 85 Main Street, Watertown, MA 02172 • (617) 926-0329
All rights reserved, including the right of reproduction in whole or in part in any form.
Printed in Italy by STIGE Turin
(sc) 10 9 8 7 6 5 4   (hc) 10 9 8 7 6 5 4 3 2

Charlesbridge

If you look underwater on any of the coral reefs of the world, you will see an incredibly beautiful place. Wow! Coral reefs may be the most interesting places on earth. A coral reef is made of millions of animals called coral. Corals have hard skeletons that attach to each other forming huge colonies. A coral colony can be almost any shape, and many different colonies form a reef.

Hundreds of other creatures live among the corals. There are seaweeds, sponges, crabs, anemones, snails, fanworms, and many more. The most colorful creatures living on the coral reefs may be the fishes . . .

Aa

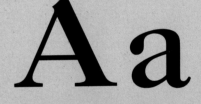

A is for Angelfish. There are enough different kinds of Angelfish in the world for someone to write an Angelfish Alphabet Book. The one on this page is a Flame Angelfish. It looks like the flame on a candle.

Bb

B is for Basslet.
Baby eagles are
called eaglets, baby
pigs are called piglets,
but baby bass are not
called Basslets. Basslets are little fish that are
different from bass. Here we have a Candy-striped
Basslet, a Blackcap Basslet, a Fairy Basslet, and
two Orange Fairy Basslets.

Cc

C is for Cowfish. Moo! Don't be silly. Cowfish do not moo, but some people think that they look like cows with horns. A Cowfish has bony plates on the outside of its body. You could say that this fish lives inside its own box!

D d

D is for Dolphin.
A Dolphin is a
mammal that
breathes air
through the
blowhole on
the top of
its head.

Dolphins are
considered one
of the smartest
creatures in
the ocean.
Remember,
these Dolphins
are not fish.

D d

D is also for Dolphin.
Is this a mistake?
No, it's not!
There is also a
fish called a Dolphin.
In Spanish, it
is called
a Dorado.
D could also
be for Dorado.
In Hawaii it is called a
Mahi-mahi. Dorados have been
known to smash their heads into
the life rafts of people lost at sea.

E e

E is for Eagle Ray.
Eagle Rays swim by flapping their wing-like fins.
Rays are related to sharks. Rays and
sharks do not have bones in their bodies.
Their skeletons are made of cartilage.
Your ears are also made of cartilage!

Ff

F is for Four-eyed Butterfly Fish. This fish does not really have four eyes. It has two eyes just like other fish, but it also has two fake eyes. Its real eye is hidden by a black line running across the side of its face. The fake eye may make its enemies think it is going where it has already been.

Gg

G is for Grunt. When Grunts are in or even out of the water, they make little grunt sounds. Grunt, grunt, grunt, oink, grunt. Grunts sometimes look like they are kissing. Maybe they are kissing. No kissing is allowed in this book.

H h

H is for
Hammerhead
Shark.
Hammerheads
have been known
to travel long
distances in large
groups. They do
not stay on coral
reefs, but they do visit because
there are so many fish there.
A shark can detect another
fish by the electrical current made in the other fish's body.

H is also for Humu-humu-nuku-nuku-apuaa. These fish make nests on the bottom of the ocean. The Humu-humu-nuku-nuku-apuaa is also called a triggerfish. In Hawaii there is a popular folk song all about the Humu-humu-nuku-nuku-apuaa. Its very long name means "the fish which has a needle, has a snout, and oinks like a pig."

H h

I is for Indigo Hamlet.
The word indigo means
blue. The indigo color allows
this fish to hide in the blue ocean.
Other hamlets have different colors
and different names, but some scientists
think they are actually one kind of fish.

J is for Jackknife Fish. This fish probably got its name because it is shaped like an open jackknife. Fish make a lot of funny noises. Some fish grunt, chirp, squeal, buzz, and squeak. The Jackknife Fish croaks like a frog. Do you think any fish sing shoo-be-doo-be-doo?

Jj

There are three basic kinds of coral reefs. A fringing reef extends from the shoreline. A barrier reef is offshore. Between a barrier reef and the land is a lagoon. An atoll is a circular collection of reefs with a lagoon in the middle.

Kk

K is for King Angelfish. King Angels are territorial. They act like kings.
They do not like other King Angels in their territory. Hey, out of the way!

L l

L is for Lionfish.
Other fish and scuba divers
stay away from the Lionfish
because some of its spines are
poisonous. In different parts of the world
this fish is called a scorpionfish, a firefish,
a zebrafish, a dragonfish, and a turkeyfish.

M is for Man-o-war. This jellyfish is one of the few ocean creatures that floats on the surface. Stay away! The Man-o-war is one of the most poisonous of all jellyfish. The top of its body is shaped like a sail on a sailboat, and the wind blows it around.

Its tentacles can grow as long as a telephone pole.

M m

Nn

N is for Nudibranch. Nudibranchs are sea slugs. Slugs? Sea slugs are not fish, they are mollusks just like clams and snails. A Nudibranch is like a snail without its shell. The one on this page is crawling on red sponge. On the Great Barrier Reef near Australia, there are more than four hundred different kinds of Nudibranchs.

O is for Oldwife. The Oldwife lives in warm waters on coral reefs. It also lives in cold ocean water. Not many fish swim in both warm and cold waters. This fish has two dorsal fins on its back.

Coral reefs exist only in warm tropical waters. Reef-building corals cannot live in sea water that is too cold or too warm.

Oo

Uh-oh! There's that shark again. Yikes, it's a Great White Shark!
A baby shark is called a pup. This one is no pup!

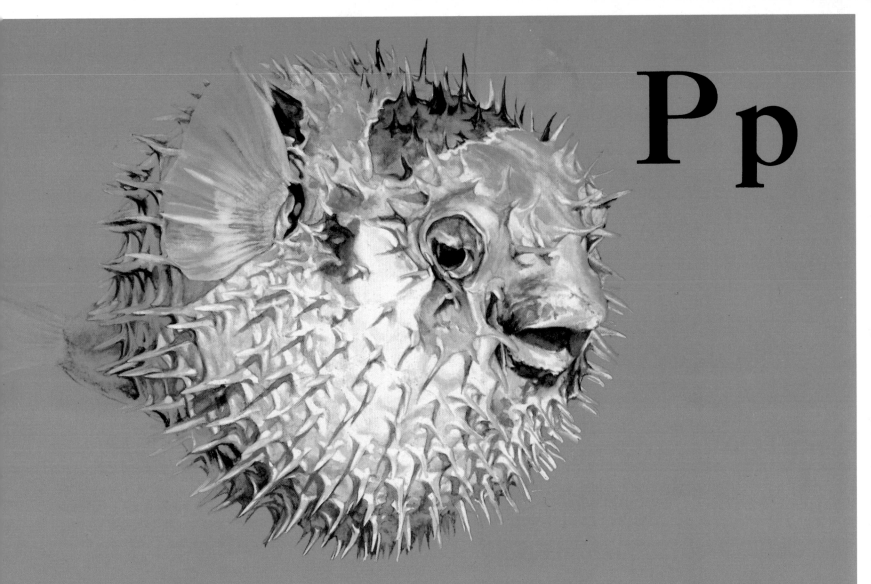

P p

P is for Porcupine Fish. The Porcupine Fish is a slow swimmer. For protection, it blows itself up into a big ball of sharp spines. Anything crazy enough to eat a Porcupine Fish is in for a surprise, and maybe a stomachache.

Q is for Queen Conch. Queen Conchs are big snails. The inside of their shells is pink and incredibly smooth. It is getting harder and harder to find Queen Conchs because people like to collect their shells. If people are not careful, pretty soon there will be no Queen Conchs left.

People everywhere have to learn to appreciate the ocean, respect the sea creatures, and do everything they can to help keep the ocean clean.

Qq

Rr

R is for Ribbon Eel. The Ribbon Eel is long and very thin like a piece of ribbon. It is so thin that it can hide in tiny crevices in rocks and coral. Baby Ribbon Eels are so clear that you can see through them. Ribbon Eel, you have a strange nose!

S s

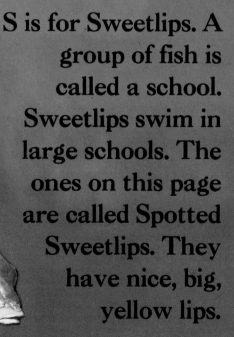

S is for Sweetlips. A group of fish is called a school. Sweetlips swim in large schools. The ones on this page are called Spotted Sweetlips. They have nice, big, yellow lips.

T is for Tomato
Clownfish. This fish makes
its home among the tentacles of
an anemone. The anemone stings and
kills other small fish, but not the Clownfish.
By staying in the tentacles, the Clownfish
is safe from other fish who might eat it.

Tt

U u

U is for Upside-down Jellyfish. Most jellyfish try to keep their domes upward and their tentacles downward. The Upside-down Jellyfish, however, goes to the bottom, flips itself over and eats upside down.

V v

V is for Veined Shrimp. It is
also called a Peppermint Shrimp
because of its bright red and white
stripes. Veined Shrimp are one
of many ocean creatures who
are cleaners. They clean the
bodies and even inside the mouths
of other fish. Most of the fish do
not eat their cleaners.
Be nice Moray Eel!

Ww

W is for Wrasse.
There are hundreds
of different kinds of
Wrasses in dozens of different
sizes, shapes, and colors. Some Wrasses
change color and shape as they grow older.

X is for Xanthidae. The crab on this page is called a Coral Crab. It is one of the crabs in the crab family Xanthidae. A crab has to shed its shell in order to grow larger. The shedding of its shell is called molting.

X x

Y y

Y is for Yellow Sea Horse. This creature is a fish, but it does not even look like a fish. It has no fins on its curly tail. It uses its tail to hold onto seaweed and coral.

Before we get to the end of the alphabet, did you know that some corals are not hard? There are soft corals such as sea fans and sea whips. On this page there is an orange sea whip.

Zz

Z is for Zebra Pipefish. Sea Horses and Pipefish are very similar. Marine biologists jokingly call a Pipefish a straightened–out Sea Horse. The Zebra Pipefish has a zillion stripes on it.

Alright, did the illustrator paint an exact mirror image of the Y page or did the printing company simply flip-flop the page?

Here's the secret. It was flip-flopped.